The Rhythm of a Woman Kingdom Style

By

Cheryl Parris

Copyright 2023 by Cheryl Parris

All rights reserved. No part of this book may be reproduced or transmitted in any form or by any means without written permission from the author.

All quotes in this book have not been created by the author, Cheryl Parris.

Manufactured in the United States of America

Dedication

I am writing this book to all the precious gifts of women that are on different journeys and seasons of life. If you are just starting out, I pray this book will help you to make wise decisions and help you to remember who you are and who you belong to. If you are a woman who has been traveling a while, I pray this book will help you to finish strong by building a legacy as a Kingdom Style woman and always remember God mercy, grace, and forgiveness! We were made for a purpose and God is using us to multiply his Kingdom with wisdom and acts of kindness!

Foreword

As a faith-based author I've always been drawn to books that encourage spiritual development utilizing a practical approach. Everyone is born with a unique set of gifts and talents which can be used to enhance the quality of life of those around us. As a Christian it is especially important to be mindful of our impact on our circle of influence. I believe that everything in life is divinely ordered by God. When I connected with Cheryl our bond as kindred spirits was immediate. Throughout my life God has surrounded me with strong women of faith and Cheryl is no exception. She epitomizes a Proverbs 31 woman, and her book serves as a great accompaniment to the Bible for women to live a more fulfilled life. She has masterfully captured the essence of what it looks like to navigate the waves of life by flowing with rather than against the tides. She shares the importance of knowing who you are in Christ so you can appreciate your value; also utilizes her own life experiences as practical tools for you to grow in grace.

The issues of life can be daunting, but with the type of insightful nuggets found in Cheryl's book you'll be able to face each challenge with confidence and grace. As I was reading, it felt like having a conversation with a good friend, telling you what you need to hear instead of what you want to hear. She does it without a glimmer of judgement or criticism. Oftentimes as women we struggle with self-doubt, low self-esteem, and insecurities. Witnessing her vulnerability and willingness to share her struggles made her book very relatable. There's nothing more reassuring when you're going through a hard time than to hear from someone who truly understands you. Although there is no doubt her perspectives are biblically based, her applications are down to earth.

When an author sets out to write a book, they are mindful of their target audience. Cheryl's book caters to women of all walks and seasons of life. For young women it will help them to make wiser choices in life and for older women it will help further their commitment to walking into their destiny. *The Rhythm of a Woman Kingdom Style* will do just that. Whether you're a babe in Christ or have been walking with Him for a long time, the principles she shares will still work. The reason they work is because they are rooted in the Word which never returns to you void. Cheryl shares her testimony of how her relationship with Christ changed the trajectory of her life and has enabled her to live a life of purpose and fulfillment. She is operating in her gift and leaving a legacy of hope for all who will listen. When she wrote this book, she understood her assignment.

Life lessons are not just for the individual that experiences them. The lessons are designed to showcase to others what God can do. As women we share a special bond and those who get that understand the importance of lifting one another up through our faith. If you want to live a more abundant life, this book should be a part of your arsenal. One of my greatest take-aways from her book is that you cannot live an abundant life and experience what pure joy really feels like unless you know who you are in Christ. Only when you embrace your identity as a child of the King can you possess the rhythm of a Kingdom Style Woman.

Deacquanita Renee Brown, Author

Faith2Inspire ~ A Journey from Pain to Purpose

Letter to the Reader

Most of you have heard that common mantra, "You see my glory, but you don't know my story". All of us have a story, others don't know about the details and most never will, but we all have been through some things.

I know what it is like to experience, low self-esteem, not knowing my value who I was in Christ before I left my parents' house and set foot into the world. I know how stressful it can be in an unequally yolk marriage which can then cause emotional and physical problems, in which can then lead to separation and divorce, and everything else that goes with that. Let me be clear about this, ALL OF US ARE CAPABLE OF THINGS THAT ARE NOT RIGHT IF WE DO NOT HAVE THE HOLY SPIRIT GUIDING US TO DO WHAT IS RIGHT! I know how it feels to be a single parent, and the death of your parents and other loved ones. The journey as a woman also included some health issues and financial challenges. I also know how my marriage to a godly husband, being a proud grandparent, and having bonus sons in a blended family brought more joy to my life. After receiving my master's degree as a nonconventional student, it afforded me to have an amazing career and enjoy life to the fullest as well. Even with the joys of life there will always be challenges as well as blessings. I only share this with you to let you know I am aware that the struggle of life is REAL, but at the same time it is so rewarding, if you position yourself right. Hopefully you will read my first book called **"Living on the Positive Side of IF"** which is a basic framework of how to live an abundant life here on earth and where you will spend eternity depending on the choices you make in ten steps. That book is for male and female. You will also see why I consider the word "IF" so powerful!

No matter what you face in life, I know beyond a shadow of doubt when you belong to the Kingdom of God, He is with you always, He will carry you when you need to be picked up. He will comfort and guide you, also don't forget, He CHOSE you. He is also a forgiving and merciful God. So, no matter what mistakes you have made, sins you have committed, God truly loves you. He is also a forgiving God! Matthew 6:33-34 are my foundation scriptures for LIFE!

When you do things God's way, life will take you higher than you ever thought possible. If I had not gone through any of my specific experiences, I would not be able to give you the wisdom of what I have learned. You will experience disappointments, joy, laughter, blessings and so many other feelings and emotions on this journey called life. However, when you have the rhythm of a Kingdom Style woman, you will move with the ebb and flow within the grace of God, which you need to navigate life.

All of us are in one of these three phases of life:

Phase One, Ladies who are just **"Starting Out"**

Phase Two, Ladies that have tried it their way and it may not be working out or just tired, so they need a **"Reset"**

Phase Three, Ladies who have traveled this life journey for a while and want to **"Finish Strong"**

What phase are you in?

The Rhythm of being a Woman!

What does rhythm mean in simple terms? The placement of sounds in time as it is regarded to music. I think of a woman like that, because she knows how to present herself in whatever situation she is in. She moves with the flow of life, the good, the bad and everything else in between. I love being a woman!

If you are not already a Kingdom Style Woman, it is one of the greatest positions to be in. Your starting point is to accept the gift of salvation. You will then have a covered life to deal with all the challenges that will face you on this journey. There is no way around it, you will still have trouble in your life, but you will also have abundant joy, grace, favor, and blessings. Also, an all-powerful, all seeing, all present and all-knowing God that is with you constantly.

Contents

Chapter 1   What is the purpose of a woman in the first place? -10

Chapter 2   How can women of today incorporate the wisdom of older women?   14

Chapter 3   How do women manage emotions with all the anxiety in the world?   17

Chapter 4   Do Kingdom Women realize the power of changing their Circle of Influence?   20

Chapter 5   How do women prepare for future hurts and still come out stronger than before they encountered those challenges?   23

Chapter 6   There is nothing wrong in looking good, but is that all there is?   26

Chapter 7   When you decide to date!   30

Chapter 8   The melody of sharing your life!   34

Chapter 9   Preparing for your latter years!   38

Chapter 10   Communication is a key factor!   42

Chapter 11   Your mind can be your worst enemy if you allow it!   45

Chapter 12   In Closing!   48

One

What is the purpose of a woman in the first place?

In most cases you may hear that God created woman to be a help meet for a man. Before you go there, I want to set the foundation for why He created any of us. Isaiah 43:7 states; Everyone who is called by my name, whom I created for my glory, whom I formed and made." As you can see, he made you for his glory, all of us. Now for a specific purpose regarding you as a woman, you are a gift to men. He wants you to be a help meet to our men. You are not a slave, but a blessing to enhance the lives of our men. There are a multitude of ways how you bless our men, please notice that I say men because everybody is not married. You may be a mother of sons, or have brothers, as well as having relatives that are males. The power of a woman is soothing, comforting and empowering only if you use it to uplift and not tear down, and to encourage.

To keep this in the form of "Kingdom Style" God made it so that a woman and a man would marry and have children within that union. Some couples get married, and they don't have children and only them and God knows why. I'm just saying this is the original God given plan. In real life, people in the world are changing so much, but God's word does not change.

Whatever your situation is, whether you are married and want or don't want children God is going to bless you with his grace if you are connected to him. Sometimes God knows that you will be a blessing to other children whether in adoption, mentoring, teaching and just loving on children that you have not birthed.

As we can see in the world today there are so many that are refusing God's original plan. You live in a world now, (that to be real about it), both parents must work, households are being neglected because the woman has so many roles to perform as a wife, mother, employee, and all the other multiple parts she plays. This is just the way society is now, it doesn't mean that it is right, but just know this was not the way it was supposed to be.

In life, you will have desires of your own, but truly sometimes it doesn't match up as to what God desires for you. When you are on the same page as him, I guarantee you, his grace is sufficient.

God already knew how it would be now and, in the future, because He is God! So being a Proverbs 31 woman seems like to me, it is truly taking place when a woman is living in a Kingdom Style manner. You have a rhythm about you to be all things to who needs you, and to be what they need at that time.

Therefore, it is so important that a woman builds herself up with daily affirmations. To deal with so many roles you need to stay connected with God. Remember this is a Kingdom Style woman.

Proverbs 31:25-31 Strength and dignity are her clothing, and she laughs at the time to come. She opens her mouth with wisdom and the teaching of kindness is on her tongue. She looks well to the ways of her household and does not eat the bread of idleness. Her children rise and call her blessed; her husband also, and he praises her. Many women have done excellently but you surpass them all. Charm is deceitful and beauty is vain but a woman who fears the Lord is to be praised. Give her of the fruit of her hands and let her works praise her in the gates.

What should a woman know before leaving her childhood home?

Have some idea of who you are! When you don't know what you believe in and who you are, you will most likely fall for anything! What are your beliefs, what kind of morals do you have? There will be many things that will test your beliefs and your character once you leave home.

When I left home, I knew I belong to God, I knew my morals, but I did not know my value.

There is always the possibility that your beliefs will change. Once you leave the familiar, you will really start to find out WHO YOU ARE! Your environment will always have a way to influence how you think.

What basic skills do you have? There will be so many things that you will learn after you leave your family. You want to know the basics like how to take care of yourself or who to call when you need help; especially in this modern society you live in today. Can you cook, and wash clothes and all the other things to be able to take care of yourself? Also do you know how to eat right and exercise so you can have healthy physical and emotional health?

Where are you going? This is regarding your education, starting your own business, military, and college among so many other choices. When you are preparing yourself regarding how you will make money in the future this is a major step towards self-sufficiency. You don't want to be waiting for someone to come "save you" from not being able to live and take care of yourself first.

I know that if I had not wanted to beat the ticking clock on when a woman is supposed to get married according to society, I would have been another journalist such as Barbara Walters, who was popular during my early years.

Rock Steady with this foundation! Now you have something to work with. You have options! Make wise choices! You don't have to accept someone or something that you don't want. You may not have the job you want right now, but you can build upon that until your change comes. "When you start seeing your worth, you'll find it harder to stay around people who don't".

You now know your purpose and you know what is important as a foundation in this vast world that we live in. The next set of statements will be food for thought to build your wisdom as a Kingdom Style woman.

IF you do these things:

1. Have a good spiritual foundation to help you to navigate through life.
2. Know where you are going regarding school, your own business, employment etc.

3. Know how to take care of yourself in all aspects of life.

Quotes that have made a deposit in my personal life.

Study while others are sleeping

Decide while others are delaying

Prepare while others are daydreaming

Begin while others are procrastinating

Work while others are wishing

Save while others are wasting

Listen while others are talking

Smile while others are frowning

Persist while others are quitting.

Two

How can women of today incorporate the wisdom of older women?

First, allow me to say this, all older women do not present themselves in a Kingdom Style manner. Their lives do not exemplify being a voice or an example for the rhythm to move through life with grace and style. Let me be clear, this does not mean that all older women have not made mistakes, or poor choices. All of this is a part of learning the journey called "life" the same as what younger women are going through now.

However, it is a bad thing to see older women judge the younger women; if someone looked in their closet there would be some things, they would not want anybody to know, but God knows. I don't want it where the younger cannot come to the older women for wisdom. All generations can learn from and need each other.

Here is a quote I love to express: "It is a wise man that learns from his mistakes, but it is a wiser man that learns from the mistakes of others".

Titus 2:4-5 ESV And so train the young women to love their husbands and children, to be self-controlled, pure, working at home, kind, and submissive to their own husbands that the word of God may not be reviled.

"Listen to your elders. Not because they're always right ... But they have more experience at being wrong".

For those of you that cannot tolerate the word "submissive" it does not mean being a "slave" to your husband. This is what a wife will do voluntary. It is a God-driven desire to please your husband and act under his authority just as Christians are to act under the authority of the church. Also, therefore it is very important to be equally yoked when you get married.

Older women can share their personal stories with younger women on how God's grace and mercy brought them through their storms. Older women can tell them what really matters in life because the world is so full of distractions. They can tell them that just because something is good does not mean it is good for them or at this time.

The seasoned women can teach how important it is to spend time with God so that you can hear his voice and how he speaks to you specifically. These women can be a comfort when the younger women are going through storms that seems like they feel are the worst things to happen in their lives.

Sometimes younger women do not realize that some closed doors can be a blessing for a bigger opportunity. There are some doors that close because of you not preparing or procrastination on your part.

When we as older women share our testimonies, it provides wisdom on how to navigate through life without making some of the same mistakes. Younger women need to know when life seems mundane, the struggles, the emotional battles, the addictions, all the major challenges in life how we came through. If it was not for God's mercy and his grace, My, My, My!

Most older women can tell you that it was nothing that they did on their own, however they had to choose to listen to the Holy Spirit speak to them. And sometimes when they didn't listen, there were consequences, but thank God for his mercy. He knows what you were going to do before you even came into this world.

IF you do these things:
1. Have a listening ear to what the older women have to say!
2. Realize just because the world is more modern, always know that some things stay in place no matter what year it is.
3. Know you will have your own experiences; however, you can save a lot of heartache by not repeating the same mistakes as others.

Quotes that have made a deposit in my personal life.

"If you want to lead you need to grow. Good leaders are always good learners". -John C. Maxwell

"I'm stronger because I had to be. I'm smarter because of my mistakes, happier because of the sadness I've known and now wiser because I've learned".

"Don't say the first thing that pops into your head, have a little bit of a (self) edit function, that's good advice for life". – Barak Obama

"Two things define you. Your patience when you have nothing, and your attitude when you have everything".

Listen to your elders. Not because they're always right ... But they have more experience at being wrong.

Know your worth. You must find the courage to leave the table if respect is no longer being served!

Starve your distractions. Feed your focus.

Three

How do women manage emotions with all the anxiety in the world?

I will tell you this as a woman, with all our hormones, our minds, our families, and outside environment it is very challenging dealing with our emotions. In the word it states that you walk by faith and not by sight. When you see or hear things that are terrible, you can get shook up quick. Your feelings can go from ten to zero in an instant. Now you know why I said earlier you must depend on the word of God. If you move away from that, you will be messed up. You will not have the wisdom of knowing that you are not your feelings.

Proverbs 3:5 states: Trust in the Lord with all your heart, and do not lean on your own understanding.

Proverbs 28:26 states: Whoever trusts in his own mind is a fool, but he who walks in wisdom will be delivered.

You need to realize that your feelings can be influenced by others and circumstances. Don't believe something because of how it makes you feel, but what the word of God states.

It is so important to set boundaries on the voices you allow to come into your life. Do you know that you can be in a conversation with someone, and they can drop one little seed and you can focus on that for hours? If you meditate on the wrong thing it will influence the decisions that you make based on your feelings. I have a very hard time being around negative people but sometimes it is good to remind me how not to be and to pour positivity into their life.

You will face anxiety, offenses, challenges and so many other things and knowing how to manage your emotions is crucial. Speaking less and listening more is an important skill to develop if you don't do it already.

By now as you can see so far it is a rhythm to being a kingdom style woman. You can't allow your flesh to dictate to you on what to say, to do, to eat, and to feel. You will wind up with broken relationships, doing more sinful things, eating too much which will affect your health and because you feel a certain way you may miss out on major opportunities.

Proverbs 12:15 states; The way of a fool is right in his own eyes: but he that hearkeneth unto counsel is wise.

1 John 3:20 states; For if our heart condemns us, God is greater than our heart, and knoweth all things.

1 John 2:15 Love not the world, neither the things that are in the world. If any man loves the world, the love of the father is not in him.

1 Corinthians 3:16 Know ye not that ye are the temple of God, and that the spirit of God dwelleth in you?

When I think back over my life journey, I was all over the place with emotions. You truly must listen more than you talk and remember once you say something, you can't take it back. You can say you are sorry, but it has already been said. There are a lot of things you do out of your feelings. Have you heard tag line such as "If it feels good, DO IT? Ladies, that is not Kingdom Style! You have a rhythm to your steps, a flow to your words and your emotions. You know who you are, you know who is in control.

I love saying this mantra as I matured in years "Lord your will, your way, and your time! He has commanded you not to worry but to pray and bring him your concerns.

IF you do these things:
1. Know you are not your feelings, because they can go up and down.
2. Realize emotions and anxiety are a part of this stressful world, you must decide how to manage them.

3. Set boundaries on what you allow to come into your mind, if not you will focus on the wrong things and do things you had not planned to do!
4. No matter what it looks like, TRUST GOD!

Quotes that have made a deposit in my personal life.

There is no greater wealth in this world than peace of mind!

Never feel guilty for setting boundaries to protect your peace.

Take life day by day and be grateful for the little things. Don't get stressed over what you can't control.

Don't let your bad days trick you into thinking you have a bad life.

Four

Do Kingdom Women realize the power of changing their circle of influence?

Over the course of my life, I heard that women can be manipulative. We all have seen examples on television and in movies as well as "real life" how women can master the skill of manipulation. Also, men can manipulate as well.

Since this book is about the rhythm of a woman kingdom style, let me just say this; God knows the motive behind everything you do. It has been said that female manipulation tricks when it comes to men are legendary to get what they want.

As I said earlier, we as women have power to build up or to tear down, to make a deposit or a withdrawal in the life of another. We must be careful on being false just to obtain the goals we want to achieve. Did you know there is a skill of good manipulation when you are trying to build up someone not with flattery but with motivation to influence another to keep going?

Sometimes women try to change another by "buttering them up to get their way, or just having selective memory about a conversation they no longer want to remember. Another way that a woman can manipulate is to use guilt trips to force one to do what they want. Also, we as women can use withdrawal in so many areas to make things happen the way we want them to or to get the attention we desire. Let's be real, most have done this, we are human.

As you grow into the ways of a kingdom woman, you learn more and more to walk in the spirit of God so that you can change your circle of influence by your actions without you even realizing it.

Galatians 5:19-23 states; Now the works of the flesh are evident: sexual immorality, impurity, sensuality, idolatry, sorcery, enmity, strife, jealousy, fits of anger, rivalries, dissensions, divisions, envy, drunkenness, orgies, and things like these. I warn you, as I warned you before, that those who do such things will not inherit the kingdom of God. But the fruit of the Spirit is love, joy, peace, patience, kindness, goodness, faithfulness, gentleness, self-control; against such things there is no law. ...

Now this is what you should strive to walk in, speak in, move in, and influence with the fruit of his Spirit.

There are so many ways that you can empower and influence your circle of influence. One way is teaching your families, serving others in church and your community, and using your voice for change. You must remember that what you do no matter how small, there are others that are watching.

In a world where social media is a powerful force you must be careful what will follow you in your later years. There are women today that would love to do more but other people are waiting to pull up on social media some things that have been done in your earlier years. Now some people do not care about this but if you want to be a kingdom woman think about things all the way through before you do them. There may be some consequences of your choices in your earlier years that will affect your future.

The big picture is this, be very careful of your choices in your early years. Most of us have made some poor choices, but as I said before God already knew you may exit off the main highway.

Mistakes, poor choices, and experience help you in your growth through life. However, some things that you choose to do can make you have future long term regrets.

So, all that you do can change your circle of influence for the good or bad. You can use your poor choices as a teaching tool when needed and to whom may need your testimony.

IF you do these things:

1. Don't use manipulation to get what you want. Be up front about what you mean. Mean what you say and say what you mean.
2. Strive to walk in the Spirit of God as much as possible. We can't do this on our own so ask the Holy Spirit to help you.
3. Make wise choices early in life so you can limit your regrets.
4. Realize that when you think not, others are watching what you say and do.

Quotes that have made a deposit in my personal life.

<u>8 things to quit</u>

1. Trying to please everyone – stopped that a long time ago
2. Fearing change
3. Living in the past
4. Overthinking – still working on this
5. Being afraid to be different
6. Sacrificing your happiness for others – If I ain't happy how can I make you happy
7. Thinking you're not good enough
8. Working until you're burnt out

Ten years from now, make sure you can say that you chose your life, you didn't settle for it.

Don't say the first thing that pops into your head, have a little bit of a (self) edit function, that's good advice for life. – Barak Obama

Five

How do women prepare for future hurts and still come out stronger than before they encountered these challenges?

Let me be clear when I say this and have some word to back it up! In this life, no matter how much you try to prepare, have plan A and B ready, you will have some hurts, heartaches, and challenges on this journey in some areas. That's a fact whether you are a kingdom woman or not. When you belong to the King, his grace will take you through. When you can't figure it out, his direction will get you there. When you think there is no way he will show you, his way!

1 Peter 4:12-13 it states, Beloved, do not think it strange concerning the fiery trial, which is to try you, as though some strange thing happened to you; But rejoice insofar as you share Christ's sufferings, that you may also rejoice and be glad when his glory is revealed.

Remember we are talking about a kingdom style woman that thinks like this.

We have heard so many people talk about difficulties, trials, and tribulations. Talking about it and going through it is two different things. It is so important that you treat others the way you want to be treated because you don't know what they are going through. At that time, they are your circle of influence and what you do and say can either make or break them.

We all have our times when it rains and storms in our household so be careful how you talk about the situation of others when you don't know what is behind the scenes. To prepare, you must spend time with the Lord and load up with word for your heart.

Proverbs 4:23 states; Guard your heart above all else, for it determines the course of your life.

You don't know what is waiting for you down the road and around the corner. On this journey of life, I didn't know what was waiting on me.

Through all the challenges I have had in life, God brought me through. I'm stronger, wiser, and so grateful for God's faithfulness, grace, and mercy.

      Early on as I was informing you to have a good strong foundation, this was my reason for saying that. Therefore, you must be fully dressed so you can do battle.

Ephesians 6:10-18 states; Finally, my brethren, be strong in the Lord, and in the power of his might. Put on the whole armor of God, that ye may be able to stand against the wiles of the devil. For we wrestle not against flesh and blood, but against principalities, against powers, against the rulers of the darkness of this world, against spiritual wickedness in high places. Wherefore take unto you the whole armor of God, that ye may be able to withstand in the evil day, and having done all, to stand. Stand therefore, having your loins girt about with truth, and having on the breastplate of righteousness; And your feet shod with the preparation of the gospel of peace; Above all, taking the shield of faith, wherewith ye shall be able to quench all the fiery darts of the wicked. And take the helmet of salvation, and the sword of the Spirit, which is the word of God: Praying always with all prayer and supplication in the Spirit and watching thereunto with all perseverance and supplication for all saints.

      The older I became, I truly understood the essence of this, when people offend you, it is not them, but the evil spirit is using them as well as you sometimes to say and do things that are not right. When you recognize that, you can forgive more easily and not judge.

      There are so many women that would just rather fight on their own and eventually find out that they can't win. When you are a kingdom woman the "fight is already fixed" and you are a winner. Remember, no matter what it looks like, just TRUST GOD!

      Depending on what age you are as you read this book, you most likely have witnessed older women giving their testimony about the goodness of the Lord. Well, this is the reason why, because they have truly experienced quite a few things in their lives, and they just want to tell somebody about what God has done for them! Don't worry, just keep on living and you will understand after a while. You have probably heard that as well. LOL

IF you do these things:

1. Know that no matter how much you plan, you will have challenges in life.
2. Prepare with your armor and your trust in God as a kingdom woman.
3. Be ready to ask God what you should learn out of your experience.
4. Celebrate and be thankful that you will be stronger, wiser and know God better.

Quotes that have made a deposit in my personal life.

<u>Forgive Yourself:</u>

- *For the times you disappointed yourself.*
- *For the times you were in the wrong.*
- *For the times you feel like you weren't enough.*
- *For the things you said out of anger.*
- *For the past mistakes you've made.*
- *For the times you could have been more empathic.*
- *For the times you've realized you were the toxic one.*
- *For the lessons you learned a little too late.*
- *For the times you didn't stand up for yourself.*

Within you is the power to rise above any situation or struggle, and transform into the Brightest, Strongest version of you EVER!!!!

To find peace, you must find courage and be willing to lose connection with the people, places and things that create all the noise in your life.

It isn't where you come from; it's where you're going that counts. – Ella Fitzgerald

Six
There is nothing wrong in looking good, but is that all there is?

It is amazing how we can make ourselves even more beautiful than we are already naturally! The clothes, the hair, cosmetic surgeries and so many other things that we can add to enhance our beauty is the normal practice in our society. I want you to understand this, you will always have someone to be interested in you, but the essence of all of this is for what reason and for how long?

It may be to your surprise or not, but there will always be someone that looks better than you naturally or with added on beauty. It is true that beauty is in the eyes of the beholder and what one person may like, another will not.

So, what does this mean for you? It means to have more to you than what meets the eyes! So many women have low self-esteem because they feel that they don't meet society's standards of beauty. Inner beauty is more important than outer beauty. Now to most women they feel that you must have something that is inviting to a man so that they can get their attention. That may be true in most cases, however it will depend on what type of attention you want.

Our society is so focused on physical beauty that so many people are using "filters" on social media to get a "like", comment etc. to help build up feelings about themselves. The one thing about that is when people see you in "real" life you may not or most likely do not look as good as the "filter" portrayed you. However, everyone must do what is best for them. Remember, my book is about The Rhythm of a Woman, Kingdom Style.

A woman's inner beauty makes it so that a man wants to be with her forever, (depending on the type of man he is). He may not know what draws him to you, but he can't get you out of his head. That is the attraction that a Kingdom woman has. Her rhythm is peaceful, encouraging, kind, gentle, smart, caring and her voice is soothing. She knows who she is, who she belongs to and does not have to be validated to know her beauty. It's nice to hear from others, but deep down inside she knows that it is the inner beauty that overpowers everything on the outside of her that looks good.

I have a strong belief that women should empower each other because we know what we go through to look good, to be what and who we need to be to others. Other women know that all of us have multiple roles that we take part in and how we manage our emotions and when we are hurt or dealing with sickness. Other women should know the different seasons women have to face when your weight goes up and down, relationships you deal with, children you are raising, careers that you are trying to build and finances you are trying to manage. So, I would advise, don't speak bad about other women, treat them the way you want to be treated. Support other women when they are trying to do something positive. The seeds you sow will always come back to you.

Looking good is wonderful, just be sure that is not all you have to offer. When you have The Rhythm of a Kingdom Woman, you glow outwardly from the reflection of you striving to walk in God's fruit of his spirit on the inside. Remember, outer beauty fades no matter what you do.

Psalms 139:13-14 For it was you who created my inward parts; you knit me together in my mother' womb. I will praise you because I have been fearfully and wonderfully made.

1 Peter 3: 3-4 Your adornment must not be merely external braiding the hair, and wearing gold jewelry, or putting on dresses; but let it be the hidden person of the heart, with the imperishable quality of a gentle and quiet spirit, which is precious in the sight of God.

Let me be clear about what I'm saying and my belief, God wants a woman to be attractive and beautiful, God already knew what men would like. However, the outer beauty should not be the only asset that she has.

Women in so many cases compare themselves to other women and it never really stops until they finally accept how God made them and enhance the natural beauty they have been given.

Also, women should realize that most women can do just like other women regarding makeup, hair, and clothes; but what stands out about you? What do you have that while other women are so focused on the physical, you are focused on what will last over time?

When you see a beautiful woman that entails the inner qualities of kindness, gentleness, thoughtfulness, and unselfishness; people can't help but want to be around her.

Proverbs 31:26 a virtuous woman is described as having the law of kindness on her tongue. This is the beauty of a Kingdom Style woman.

IF you do these things:

1. Be the best version of you and nobody else.
2. Don't compare yourself to other women as a measurement of your own beauty.
3. Build up your inner beauty, your skills, and your gift of being a Kingdom woman.
4. Know who you are and appreciate your uniqueness. That is your power!

Quotes that have made a deposit in my personal life.

Beauty is when you can appreciate yourself. When you love yourself, that's when you're most beautiful." - Zoe Kravitz.

To be beautiful means to be yourself. You don't need to be accepted by others. You need to accept yourself."

"How I feel about myself is more important than how I look. Feeling confident, being comfortable in your skin – that's what really makes you beautiful." - Bobbi Brown.

"It is not fancy hair, gold jewelry, or fine clothes that should make you beautiful. No, your beauty should come from within you - the beauty of a gentle and quiet spirit. This beauty will never disappear, and it is worth very much to God." - Peter 3:3-4, The Bible.

"No matter how plain a woman may be, if truth and honesty are written across her face, she will be beautiful." - Eleanor Roosevelt.

"Inner beauty radiates from within, and there's nothing more beautiful than when a woman feels beautiful on the inside." - Erin Heatherton.

Seven
When you decide to date!

When it comes to dating, this is serious business! Yes, it can be enjoyable, and you will learn how to socialize with the opposite sex. We all know that opposites attract, and you can be involved with someone physically before you know it and the consequences can have long term effects. Also, have a good knowledge of sexual soul ties. A sexual soul tie is that every sexual relationship results in a soul connection with the partner that you are intimate with. In marriage, a sexual soul tie is a positive force. When people are married and committing adultery, they are breaking their marriage covenant as well as allowing outside spirits into their marriage relationship.

1 Corinthians 6:14-15 Flee from sexual immorality. Every other sin a person commits is outside the body, but the sexually immoral person sins against his own body.

You must decide what you can deal with, what your weaknesses may be. It is a good practice to learn about a person for their intrinsic values to go along with their physical attractiveness.

Sometimes you may want to date to build up your self-confidence or learn how to communicate with men. So, know your "why" for dating in the beginning stages. Also remember you are a Kingdom Style woman. Men can always find women to meet and satisfy their physical desires. This book is not addressing what is wrong or right for men, I can only stay in my lane as a woman.

Now if you have reached that point in your life when you want to get married one day, you will have to have more than just the physical beauty. Therefore, I said earlier for you to be complete within yourself in how to take care of you! You will not need to have someone validate what your value is as a woman. You already know who you belong to, you already know that God design you to look and be a certain way for his purpose.

You have now reached this season in your life where you want to join in with the opposite sex to create a commitment of family.

Genesis 2:18 Then the Lord God said, "It is not good that the man should be alone; I will make him a helper fit for him."

So, while you are dating you are gathering information, checking for red flags, listening to what he says and seeing if the action matches his words. You are seeing if you two are equally yoked and compatible. Do you both put God first?   Marriage is a serious union and should not be taken likely. You need to know whether they want children, do they have unresolved family issues by holding bitterness and hatred within themselves. When you decide to marry, you will be connected to your spouse's family.

1 Corinthians 15:33 Do not be deceived; "Bad company ruins good morals."

Yes, you can enjoy the dating process, but you can't allow yourself to be complacent.

Whatever you allow before marriage will be amplified after you join in this union.

Back in the day, people would just fall in love and get married and if things didn't work out, they just stayed in it and would be miserable or just learn how to endure. Look at all the broken marriages today, even in the Christian arena. Something is wrong!

Also, some women spend years dating the same person and not moving toward a marriage commitment. Know when it is time to move on. You can be dating for all those years and then the man turns around and marries somebody else. Your years as a woman are very valuable in the sense of if you are planning to have children and your value as a woman.

2 Timothy 2:22 So flee youthful passions and pursue righteousness, faith, love, and peace, along with those who call on the Lord from a pure heart.

Matthew 19:5 And said, therefore a man shall leave his father and his mother and hold fast to his wife, and the two shall become one flesh.

Romans 12:1-2 I appeal to you therefore, brothers, by the mercies of God, to present your bodies as a living sacrifice, holy and acceptable to God which is your spiritual worship. Do not be conformed to this world, but be transformed by the renewal of your mind, that by testing you may discern what is the will of God, what is good and acceptable and perfect.

   Unfortunately, most people have not followed God's word when it comes to dating and preparing for marriage. So many couples start living together, fornication, adultery, experimenting with the same sex physically. Therefore, it is so important to heal or have counseling after being abused physically or emotionally or having low self-esteem so that you can make better choices and do what God says to do.

   There is no guarantee that your marriage union will last, even after you have done everything to the best of your knowledge. We are all in a state of becoming. If things don't go in the direction, you wanted it to, you will still survive because your foundation was strong. So many women deal with physically and/or emotionally abusive relationships because they can't survive on their own because of low wages, low self- esteem, fear of failure, health has gone bad, stress weight, etc. Therefore, you must maintain "YOU" while in a marriage relationship and raising children. You don't want to lose yourself and try to pour from an empty cup.

   If you must, start over again, it is okay to be alone to get yourself back on track. You may be alone but not lonely. Seek God for direction, because this may be a vulnerable time and you don't want to latch on to a man, just so you can say you have a man.

   It is good to know what season of life you are in and self-evaluate your life to see if you are going to be obedient to God's word to the best of your ability. God knows we are not perfect. However, if we leave our behavior up to ourselves, we will be headed for a great disaster. There are men waiting for the woman who wants a man so bad that she will ignore the "red flags" just to meet her needs physically.

   In most cases all a man must do is just listen as a woman talks and he will know exactly what to say and do to get her on his side. She can wind up taking care of him, giving him money and so many other things. We need the guidance of the Holy Spirit. Remember this book is for a Kingdom style woman.

1 John 2:16 For all that is in the world, the desires of the flesh and the desires of the eyes and pride in possessions, is not from the Father, but is from the world.

IF you do these things:

1. When you decide you want to date, know your reasons for doing so.
2. Make sure to have a good understanding of sexual soul ties.
3. When deciding you want to be married, don't date for just a good feeling. Be intentional on who and what you want. Date with a PURPOSE!
4. Truly ask the Holy Spirit to guide you and remember do your best to be living in a Kingdom style manner.
5. Maintain your identity, your mind and body and your skills so if marriage does not work out, you have not lost yourself totally.

Quotes that have made a deposit in my personal life.

Keep your distance from people who will never admit they are wrong and who always try to make you feel like it's your fault.

Accept responsibility for your actions. Be accountable for your results. Take ownership of your mistakes.

We don't grow when things are easy. We grow when we face challenges.

Eight

The melody of sharing your life!

It is one thing trying to learn about yourself and you will never know you the way God knows you. When you start sharing your life with a husband, children, your career, taking care of yourself, you will be having multiple roles. You will also be connected to your parents, in-laws, church, and community. For all the roles that you carry daily, there will be joyful times as well as challenges.

You will have to take an active role in self-care so that you can serve others with the best of your ability. When you are a woman, you have natural monthly challenges as well as hormonal physical challenges with age. As a Kingdom style woman, you will need to spend time in God's word and prayer so that you can communicate and balance your life for abundance.

There are so many distractions in our world today that it can be easy to focus on the wrong thing and you can shortchange your family and yourself.

Your children will go through different development stages, and you must be in tune with them. Also knowing how to hear your husband in what he speaks and what he doesn't say. You will be empowered by obtaining positive knowledge on how to communicate and understand your different roles.

When it comes to family you want to make should that there is communicated love, mutual respect, constant encouragement and have time for fun.

The Woman who fears the Lord!

¹⁰ [d] An excellent wife who can find?
She is far more precious than jewels.
¹¹ The heart of her husband trusts in her,
and he will have no lack of gain.
¹² She does him good, and not harm,
all the days of her life.
¹³ She seeks wool and flax,
and works with willing hands.
¹⁴ She is like the ships of the merchant;
she brings her food from afar.
¹⁵ She rises while it is yet night
and provides food for her household
and portions for her maidens.
¹⁶ She considers a field and buys it;
with the fruit of her hands she plants a vineyard.
¹⁷ She dresses herself[e] with strength
and makes her arms strong.
¹⁸ She perceives that her merchandise is profitable.
Her lamp does not go out at night.
¹⁹ She puts her hands to the distaff,
and her hands hold the spindle.
²⁰ She opens her hand to the poor
and reaches out her hands to the needy.
²¹ She is not afraid of snow for her household,
for all her household are clothed in scarlet.[f]
²² She makes bed coverings for herself;
her clothing is fine linen and purple.
²³ Her husband is known in the gates
when he sits among the elders of the land.

²⁴She makes linen garments and sells them;
she delivers sashes to the merchant.
²⁵ Strength and dignity are her clothing,
and she laughs at the time to come.
²⁶ She opens her mouth with wisdom,

> and the teaching of kindness is on her tongue.
> ²⁷ She looks well to the ways of her household
> and does not eat the bread of idleness.
> ²⁸ Her children rise up and call her blessed;
> her husband also, and he praises her:
> ²⁹ "Many women have done excellently,
> but you surpass them all."
> ³⁰ Charm is deceitful, and beauty is vain,
> but a woman who fears the LORD is to be praised.
> ³¹ Give her of the fruit of her hands,
> and let her works praise her in the gates.

The Proverbs 31 woman in the bible did so many things and in the world today it seems like you are wearing all those hats as well. You will have to have a rhythm to manage the awesome position of sharing your life with others. Therefore, it is so important to try to stay physically and emotionally healthy. You are the heartbeat of the family.

Psalm 128:3 "Your wife will be like a fruitful vine within your house; your children will be like olive shoots around your table."

Proverbs 22:6 "Train up a child in the way he should go; even when he is old, he will not depart from it."

IF you do these things:

1. Spend time in prayer and read God's word to know how to manage your household.
2. Learn to be in tune with your husband and your children through the different seasons of their lives as well as your own.
3. Self-care is very important. You can't pour from an empty cup.
4. Realize that as a woman with multiple roles, you are the heartbeat of the family.

Quotes that have made a deposit in my personal life.

Respect is like a mirror, the more you show it to other people, and the more they will reflect it back.

5 Rules to Live a Happier Life:

1. Love Yourself, 2. Do Good, 3. Harm No One, 4. Be Positive, 5. Always Forgive

Nine

Preparing for your latter years!

If you keep living, you will enter your latter years where you can have a chance to look back over your life with regrets or a since of contentment because you have blessed others. Memories are happening which can be good and bad. You must be intentional on the seeds that you have sown to be good seeds. As I have said in my first book **"Living on the Positive Side of IF"** you can make choices and decisions, but **if** you don't act, a decision will be made by default.

Therefore, being around different family members, friends, and coworkers, is so important that you know people have different perspectives and that is their reality. When communicating with adult children, it is good to remember that the choices, they make are their own choices, not yours. All you want to do is, when you interact with them, just respect their decision and if they want your opinion, you be there as a consultant only. You will realize that there is a time that you must **Let Go**, and **Let God** do what he does.

In this season of life, you want to make sure that you have your necessary paperwork. For example: Will, trust, Long Term care and insurance documents and a location for all paperwork to be found by you or others. All of this is so important in case you are sick or no longer living; it will make it less stressful for your family. Ask yourself the questions below:

What do you have in place for living arrangements if you are the survivor of your marriage or no longer married and it is just you?

Are you going to live with your children or by yourself?

How are your finances for now and long-term living because none of us know our expiration date?

Are you eating right, exercising with cardio and resistance training so you can have strength for a better quality of life?

Are you enjoying this season of your life because you have prepared for an abundant harvest of family, a personal relationship with Jesus and relaxing in your seasoned years?

Have you brought closure to unresolved issues, any unforgiveness to a person that needs to be forgiven?

Do you have any favorite scriptures that you can share with others or testimonies to help the next generation to stay grounded? Also, you can share the lessons that you have learned in life so far as well. Write them down so they will have personal stories.

I have a book to enter information about you called **"Your Life Story"** sold on Amazon so you can have a location of an overview of your life journey and a place to give advice to the younger generation as a legacy journal.

WOMAN

When God created woman, he was working late on the 6th day.......
An angel came by and asked." Why spend so much time on her?" Lord answered. "Have you seen all the specifications I have to meet to shape her?"

- She must function in all kinds of situations.
- She must be able to embrace several kids at the same time.
- Have a hug that can heal anything from a bruised knee to a broken heart.
- She must do all this with only two hands
- She cures herself when sick and can work 18 hours a day.

THE ANGEL was impressed" Just two hands.....impossible!
And this is the standard model?" The Angel came closer and touched the woman. "But you have made her so soft, Lord".
"She is soft", said the Lord, " But I have made her strong. You can't imagine what she can endure and overcome"
"Can she think?" The Angel asked...
The Lord answered. "Not only can she think, but she can also reason and negotiate". The Angel touched her cheeks....
"Lord, it seems this creation is leaking! You have put too many burdens on her". "She is not leaking...it is a tear". The Lord corrected the Angel...
"What's it for?" Asked the Angel...... .
The Lord said. "Tears are her way of expressing her grief, her doubts, her love, her loneliness, her suffering and her pride."...
This made a big impression on the Angel,
"Lord, you are a genius. You thought of everything.
A woman is indeed marvelous"
Lord said. "Indeed she is.

- She has strength that amazes a man.
- She can handle trouble and carry heavy burdens.
- She holds happiness, love, and opinions.
- She smiles when she feels like screaming.
- She sings when she feels like crying, cries when happy and laughs when afraid.
- She fights for what she believes in.
- Her love is unconditional.
- Her heart is broken when a next-of-kin or a friend dies but she finds strength to get on with life"

The Angel asked: So, she is a perfect being?
The lord replied: No. She has just one drawback.
"She often forgets what she is worth".

- Author Unknown

Ten

Communication is a key factor!

This is an area that will be major all throughout your life. From what I have found out down through the years of my life is effective communication can take you to higher levels in life. What do I mean by that? When a person knows how to listen to others by being in tune to what the other person is trying to say. So many people don't hear others while they are talking because they are thinking about what they want to say next. Therefore, we must "actively" listen to others. People want to be heard by you.

Have you tried to have a conversation with others and their **body language** just "makes you want to stop talking"? It is so important that when people are talking to us, they know that you are in tuned with them. Now in some cases, with some people you really don't care what they are saying. Let's be real about this. However, for those important conversations, you always need to check your body language, you can't see your face, but you can feel if you are looking mad or frowning up. Negative body language will turn people off in wanting to talk with you.

Tone of your voice is a big area of focus for me. It carries so much weight in how a person receives your words, and your message. Do you realize that others may hear the volume and tone of your words and it may offend them and you don't realize why they don't want to talk to you. Therefore, being sarcastic is something that you want to be conscious of when having a meaningful conversation with another person. Sometimes you may be sarcastic to get a point across, but you know when and why. Also, some people tell you things and after they tell you they say they are joking. They already know it wasn't a joke. People should just mean what they say and say what they mean. Communication is crucial!

When you try to **understand** what a person is trying to tell you is a good skill to practice as well. So, to do that, it is good to paraphrase what you believe they are trying to tell you when it is necessary. Men and women normally talk in different ways, so it is good to have some understanding in the ways that men communicate.

How we **manage our emotions** is very important for effective communication. You can become so agitated and defensive that you don't hear nothing that the other person is trying to say and what they mean by their message delivery.

Proverbs 12:25 (ESV) "Anxiety in a man's heart weighs him down, but a good word makes him glad."

Proverbs 25:1 (ESV) "A word fitly spoken is like apples of gold in a setting of silver."

So, it is so important in how you effectively communicate with others and what you say to yourself as well.

Matthew 12:37 (ESV) "…… for by your words you will be justified, and by your words you will be condemned."

As a Kingdom Style woman, it is apparent through God's word that our behavior and actions have consequences in the Kingdom of God. Also, it is obvious that our spoken words bring ramifications. When we fill our hearts with God's word, we will be able to practice good communication. Remember, you can't do this in your own strength, we must lean on and obey the Holy Spirit to empower us.

If you do these things:

1. Be mindful of how you listen, use body language, use tone, your understanding of others and manage your emotions.
2. Remember as a Kingdom Style woman you are being shown in how you behave as a representative of God's Kingdom. You will truly learn yourself more.
3. You can't do this in your own strength, you must be empowered by the Holy Spirit.

Quotes that have made a deposit in my life.

"Ultimately the bond of all companionship, whether in marriage or in friendship, is conversation." Oscar Wilde

"The most important thing in communication is to hear what isn't being said." Peter Drucker

"Trust is the glue of life. It is the most essential ingredient in effective communication. It's the foundational principle that holds all relationships." Stephen R. Covey

"Communication to a relationship is like oxygen is to life. Without it, it dies." Tony A. Gaskins Jr.

"Conflict avoidance is not the hallmark of a good relationship. On the contrary, it is a symptom of serious problems and poor communication." Harriet B. Braiker

Eleven

Your mind can be your worst enemy!

Most likely you have heard about the battlefield of your mind, which is a true statement. What I want you to know, this will be your ongoing challenge your entire life. The more you can develop the skills to handle the mind, the better and more peaceful your life will be. All that I have mentioned in the earlier chapters are based on how you manage your mind.

Some of the areas that I have experienced and others that I have met throughout the years have gone through this as well:

We have expectations of how things are supposed to be. We don't know what will take place in our lives. We are not totally in control of our lives. We prepare, we make choices and still there is no guarantee in what the outcome will be.

You must accept reality instead of fighting it. Sometimes we allow what we expected to happen, to blind us of all the good things that is taking place in our lives. To enjoy others for who and what they truly are, you must stop expecting people and things to be perfectly the way that you had imagined.

We demolish arguments and every pretension that sets itself up against the knowledge of God, and we take captive every thought to make it obedient to Christ. 2 Corinthians 10:5

Sometimes we expect constant contentment. When you can realize this, happiness and sadness need each other. One reinforces the other. If you don't have rain, you will not appreciate sunshine in your life.

You can be your own worst critic. It is important to take self- inventory, but don't go overboard. The enemy is always going to point out and deposit negative thoughts in your head to distract you from moving forward. If you constantly over-criticize yourself, you will become stagnant and stop pressing forward. You need your confidence, so what you tell yourself is important.

There are times when you can over analyze a person or a situation. It is good to analyze but when you keep going in circles because you are dealing with your mind and your instinct, it may be challenging. Therefore, a Kingdom Style woman must pray, read the word of God and He will give you direction and peace about the situation.

Making assumptions about people and situations. In so many cases you will assume things because you don't know what is behind the scenes. You may not know the motive as to why a person is doing something or has said a certain thing to you. The enemy will always want you to think the worst. So, depending on what it is that you are assuming don't waste time on needless situations.

Your beliefs can be self-limiting. When you don't believe in yourself, you don't have any hope or faith, things will remain the same. Once you realize that your mind reflects your thoughts, your mind drives your body and the only person that can hold you down is You.

But he said to me, "My grace is sufficient for you, for my power is made perfect in weakness." Therefore, I will boast all the more gladly about my weaknesses, so that Christ's power may rest on me. That is why for Christ's sake, I delight in weaknesses, in insults, in hardships, in persecutions, in difficulties. For when I am weak then I am strong. 2 Corinthians 12:9-10

If you to these things:

1. Be mindful that you have an enemy that will deposit negative things, and half-truths in your mind center daily. You are the only one that can manage what you keep in your head.
2. You mind drives your body, what you do and how far you will go in life.
3. It will take effort and practice to build a skill of managing your thought life.
4. Use the weapons that you have been given to deal with your mind. His word and prayer.

Quotes that have made a deposit in my life:

"You only have control over three things in your life – the thoughts you think, the images you visualize, and the actions you take." Jack Canfield

"What consumes your mind is what controls your life. " Anonymous

"Control your thoughts. Decide about that which you will think and concentrate upon. You are in charge of your life to the degree you take charge of your thoughts." Earl Nightingale

"Take control of your consistent emotions and begin to consciously and deliberately reshape your daily experience of life." Tony Robbins

Twelve

In Closing!

These previous chapters have provided you with the rhythm to move and navigate through life as a Kingdom Style woman. Since all of us are passing through and realize this is not our home, we can build a strong foundation to withstand the multiple challenges of life. Even when you do all this planning and preparation, God still orders our steps. What will make it bad is when we are disobedient. We have all disobeyed God, but his grace and mercy has kept us. He is God of more than a second chance. However, let's change the narrative by just doing what He says to do whether we like it, understand it or not. Listen to the experiences of different women that come across your paths in life. If you can learn from their mistakes, you don't have to make the same ones. You will of course have your own experiences, failures, and challenges; these are the building blocks for character.

In my own life, I have gotten off the main road, but God used my experiences to empower young ladies to build a strong foundation. My parents provided that for me however I wanted to do things my way and I learned early in life to get back on the main highway. The things I mention in the early chapters of this book is to consult the Holy Spirit for guidance, have your own career, know how to take care of yourself, date with purpose, and know who you are. I had to find out these things throughout my life. I thank God for my journey, my husband, my sons and their families, my career and now to have several platforms to provide wisdom to others.

Appreciate where you are in your journey, even if it's not where you want to be. Every season serves a purpose.

The Rhythm of a Woman, Kingdom Style, does not mean that you live a boring life. It means for you to move to the beat of the different seasons you will face in life with love, laughter, and wisdom. It means that you will represent God's kingdom to the best of your ability and set an example for others. It means, you will strive to move in the fruit of the spirit such as love, joy, peace, patience, goodness, gentleness kindness, faithfulness, and self-control. It means that you are thankful for the sunshine and rain in your life, and you will praise God for everything he has blessed you with. I love being a woman, I love nurturing and empowering others. I love God and being an ambassador for his Kingdom.

New Living Translation Isaiah 61:10
I am overwhelmed with joy in the LORD my God! For he has dressed me with the clothing of salvation and draped me in a robe of righteousness. I am like a bridegroom dressed for his wedding or a bride with her jewels.

When you think about the scripture above, do you realize how expensive those garments are that he has given you? His son suffered, died, and OVERCAME death for you and me. Therefore, you want to take your role serious to have **The Rhythm of a Woman, Kingdom Style!**

So, as you have read in this book so far, it is truly all depending on what you choose as you are about to leave your family home or wherever you are at the present time. Be mindful of who gives you advice and the multiple voices that will feed your mind. You must be intentional in your life to build the life you want. Everything that looks good or is good is not for you at that time or not at all. Therefore, I constantly ask the Lord by saying: Your will, Your way, and Your time Lord! You will be inundated with all types of thoughts that will enter your mind, your emotions will try to take over, and before you know it you will act according to those thoughts. I have emptied out everything that I have learned after 70 years of life, and I now pass it on to you. All I ask, as you learn, please pass it on to others because when you sow those seeds it will come back to you; more than you sowed, and the harvest will be phenomenal. If you sow bad seeds the same principle takes place. Remember as a Kingdom woman, you don't belong to yourself, you are for the purpose of building up God's Kingdom, you are his ambassador. It is not easy, but the outcome will be so rewarding. Just drop seeds and remember people would rather see a sermon than to hear one only.

When you strive to do the best that you can while you can and fill your heart with the fruit of the spirit of God, you will do great things. **Now remember you can't do this in your own strength that is why God sent the Holy Spirit to empower you to do what is right.** We will mess up sometimes, but we get back on track and keep moving forward because this is not our home.

Remember always that God loves you, He chose you and you belong to Him.

My prayer is for you and yours to have Peace on this journey of life!

About The Author

Cheryl Parris is a wife, mother, grandmother, believer, podcast-host and so much more! She obtained a master's degree in social work and used that degree in her field until retiring years later. As an author, Cheryl is making her mark with three published titles, **"The Rhythm of a Woman, Kingdom Style" and "Living on the Positive Side of IF" as well as "Your Life Story"** (a legacy journal).   Cheryl exercises her leadership abilities in a Facebook group hosted by herself, called "Less Stress 2 Success". She lives by the quote "IF you make proactive choices, you will reduce reactive stress." This group provides a space for women and men to manage their stress levels in all areas of life. Mrs. Parris also shares her voice through her podcast, and You Tube channel which are both called "IF has Power". These two platforms are a way to provide the testimonies of others who have gone from **mess to a message.**

In her time of relaxation, she loves to travel, create legacy projects, dance, and eat at awesome restaurants. Cheryl Parris is most passionate about leaving a legacy of wisdom for others that are traveling this most challenging and rewarding journey called life and preparing others for where they will spend eternity.

If you would like to take a deep dive into more of how to navigate the different phases of a woman traveling through life, please see the link below for my course called:

Kingdom Style Woman, Life Navigation Course

Primary Goal of Course

Depending on where you are in life will be the direction in which you take steps. This course will give you the framework to help you reach your desired destination!

Please check out my website and You Tube for this course announcement.

My website: cheryparris.org

You Tube: https://www.youtube.com/@cherylparris3267

Additional Resources:

My books **"Living on the Positive Side of IF" and "Your Life Story"** can be purchased on Amazon.

Made in the USA
Columbia, SC
12 September 2024